DISCARD

Well Made, Fair Trade

My chocolate Bar

and Other Foods

W9-BUI-502

CRABTREE
Publishing Company
www.crabtreebooks.com

Crabtree Publishing Company

www.crabtreebooks.com

1-800-387-7650

Published in Canada
Crabtree Publishing
616 Welland Avenue
St. Catharines, ON
L2M 5V6

Published in the United States
Crabtree Publishing
PMB 59051
350 Fifth Ave, 59th Floor
New York, NY 10118

Author: Helen Greathead

Editorial director: Kathy Middleton

Editors: Julia Bird and Ellen Rodger

Designer: Q2A Media

Proofreader: Wendy Scavuzzo

Prepress technician: Margaret Amy Salter

Print and production coordinator: Katherine Berti

Published by Crabtree Publishing Company in 2017

All rights reserved. No part of this publication may be reproduced, stored in a retrieval system, or transmitted in any form or by any means, electronic, mechanical, photocopy, recording or otherwise, without the prior written permission of the copyright owner.

First published in 2014 by Franklin Watts
(A division of Hachette Children's Books)
Copyright © Franklin Watts 2014

Printed in Canada/072016/PB20160525

Photographs:
Front Cover: Kesu, Nicram Sabod, Ammit Jack, AlephStudio, Stockyimages, Marco mayer/Shutterstock. Back Cover: Africa924/Shutterstock. Title page: Madlen, Kesu, Troyker, Joloei, Valentyn Volkov, Evgeny Karandaev, S-F, Sunsetman/Shutterstock. Imprint Page: Picsfive, Madlen, Sunsetman, Maks Narodenko, Horiyan/Shutterstock. P4(L): Marcus Lyonss/Fairtrade Ireland, P4(R):FairTrade International; P5: Ekler/Shutterstock; P6(R): Tristan Tan/Shutterstock, P6(L): Sursad/Shutterstock; P7(T): TongChuwit/Shutterstock; P7(B): Twin Design/Shutterstock; P8(T): FairTrade International; P8(C): Divine Chocolate Ltd; P8(B): Marie-Amelie Ormieres/Max Havelaar Belgium/Fairtrade International; P9(T): Divine Chocolate Ltd; P9(B): Kim Naylor/Divine Chocolate Ltd; P10: Panom/Shutterstock; P11(T): Muriel Lasure/Shutterstock, P11(B): Paul J Martin/Shutterstock; P12 Chris Pole/Shutterstock; P13(T): Eduardo Martino/Documentography/FairTrade International; P13(B):TongChuwit/Shutterstock; P14: Daniel J. Rao/Shutterstock; P15(T): F9photos/Shutterstock; P15(B): PavelSvoboda/Shutterstock; P16(B): Clipper teas.com; P16(T): TongChuwit/Shutterstock; P16(C): FairTrade International; P17(T): Jean Luc Lucien/T'Classic (Darjeeling) Pvt. Ltd; P17(B): Matt Gibson/Shutterstock; P18: RichardThornton/Shutterstock; P19: Xuanhuongho/Shutterstock; P20(TL): Cora Mueller/Shutterstock; P20(C): Jeremy Horner/Nomad/Corbis; P20(CR): FairTrade International; P20(BR): Chooseliberation.com; P21(T): TongChuwit/Shutterstock; P21(B): Simon de trey-White; P22:Samuel Borges Photography/Shutterstock; P22-23(Bgrnd): Happystock/Shutterstock; P23(T):Hywit Dimyadi/Shutterstock; P23(B): Elena Schweitzer/Shutterstock; P24(Bgrnd): Veron_ice/Shutterstock; P24(BL): The Turtle Factory/Shutterstock; P24 (TR): FairTrade International; P24(CR): Naturalbeverages; P25: Jose Manuel Gomez/Fairtrade International; P26: Alex Staroseltsev/Shutterstock; P26-27(Bgrnd): Ramona Kaulitzki/Shutterstock; P27(B): Traidcraft; P27(T): Darios/shutterstock; P27 (C): FairTrade International; P28: Darios/shutterstock; P29(T): Felix Rohan/Shutterstock; P29(B): AndreyKlepikov/Shutterstock; P30-31(Bgrnd): Tatyana Vyc/Shutterstock; P31: Picsfive, Madlen, Sunsetman, Maks Narodenko, Horiyan/Shutterstock; P32:Olha Afanasieva/Shutterstock. Illustrations: all-free-downloads.com (P4, 10, 12, 14-15, 26)

Library and Archives Canada Cataloguing in Publication

Greathead, Helen, author
        My chocolate bar and other foods / Helen Greathead.

(Well made, fair trade)
Includes index.
Issued in print and electronic formats.
ISBN 978-0-7787-2714-9 (hardback).--
ISBN 978-0-7787-2718-7 (paperback).--
ISBN 978-1-4271-1844-8 (html)

        1. Food industry and trade--Juvenile literature. 2. Food industry and trade--Moral and ethical aspects--Juvenile literature. 3. Food industry and trade--Employees--Juvenile literature. I. Title.

HD9000.5.G72 2016   j338.1   C2016-902579-9
                                                          C2016-902580-2

Library of Congress Cataloging-in-Publication Data

Names: Greathead, Helen, author.
Title: My chocolate bar and other foods / Helen Greathead.
Description: New York : Crabtree Publishing Company, 2016. |
    Series: Well made, fair trade | "First published in 2014 by Franklin Watts." | Includes index.
Identifiers: LCCN 2016016658 (print) | LCCN 2016026194 (ebook) |
    ISBN 9780778727149 (reinforced library binding) |
    ISBN 9780778727187 (pbk.) |
    ISBN 9781427118448 (electronic HTML)
Subjects: LCSH: Fair trade foods--Juvenile literature. | Food industry and trade--Juvenile literature. | International trade--Moral and ethical aspects--Juvenile literature.
Classification: LCC HD9000.5 .G724 2016 (print) | LCC HD9000.5 (ebook) |
    DDC 174/.963--dc23
LC record available at https://lccn.loc.gov/2016016658

R0446784620

OCT 2016

Contents

Words in **bold** can be found in the glossary on page 30.

Why buy Fairtrade foods?

How often do you look at the packaging on the foods that you eat? Have you ever noticed a mark or logo that shows the product has been produced fairly, such as the FAIRTRADE Mark?

What does the FAIRTRADE Mark mean?

The FAIRTRADE Mark was first added to food products, such as cocoa, tea, and sugar, in 1994. The FAIRTRADE Mark shows that the product has been certified by the Fairtrade Foundation. The Fairtrade Foundation is a member of Fairtrade International, and its mark lets buyers know that the food has been sourced from farmers involved in Fairtrade practices. In this book, Fairtrade spelled with a capital "F" refers to Fairtrade Foundation, Fairtrade International, or FAIRTRADE Mark products.

This is a FAIRTRADE Mark. It shows that the product is certified, and the farmers and workers involved in producing it were treated fairly and were paid a fair price.

For a product to carry the FAIRTRADE Mark, its ingredients must abide by Fairtrade practices. That means the sugar in a chocolate bar, and ingredients, such as vanilla, dried fruit, or nuts, are Fairtrade, too.

How do fair trade organizations help?

Big companies make huge profits selling us food, but the small farmers and workers who produce the food often struggle to earn a living. Fair trade organizations throughout the world such as the Fairtrade Foundation in the United Kingdom, Fairtrade America, Fairtrade Canada, and the independent Fair Trade U.S.A., are non-profit groups that help farmers, **cooperatives**, and local communities in **developing countries** to build better lives and protect the environment.

This book uses many terms to describe fair trade. Here are some helpful descriptions:

fair trade Trade or the sale of food and products in which fair prices are paid to the people who produce them in developing countries

fair trade certification A guarantee that a product you buy in stores has been farmed and produced according to a fair trade organization's rules

Fairtrade Foundation A United Kingdom-based charity that helps farmers and producers get a fair deal for their work. It is a part of Fairtrade International and uses the FAIRTRADE Mark certification.

Fairtrade International An organization of producer groups and 25 fair trade organizations from around the world

Fair Trade Certified The trademark label of Fair Trade U.S.A., an independent fair trade organization in the United States.

fairly traded Some smaller independent fair trade organizations use the term "fairly traded" on their certification labels to note that their products have been traded in a fair, or ethical manner

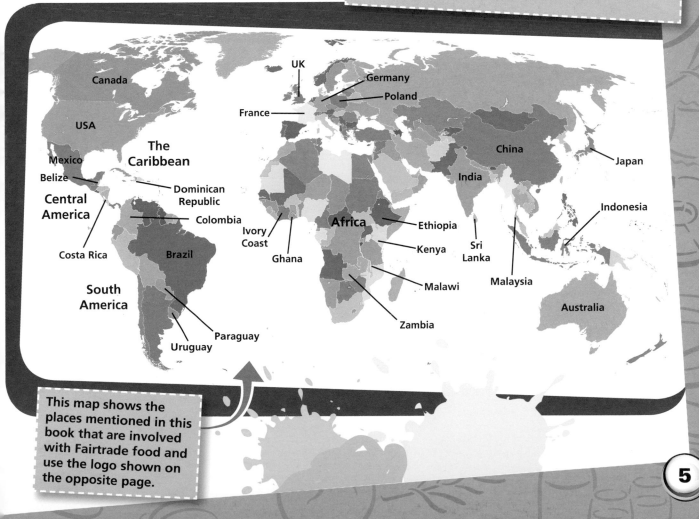

This map shows the places mentioned in this book that are involved with Fairtrade food and use the logo shown on the opposite page.

Special treatment

Many workers on cocoa plantations cannot afford health care if they become ill, and may have to travel a long way to the nearest hospital. Some do not get the treatment they need in time and they die. The Kavokiva cooperative was founded by 600 farmers in 1999, in the southeast of the Ivory Coast. Up to 30 Kavokiva farmers died each year due to injury or ill health. As well as paying a higher price for members' cocoa beans and providing financial support for **fertilizers**, pesticides, and school fees, the cooperative also pays medical expenses.

One of Kavokiva's biggest achievements has been financing its own health center with a doctor, midwife, and two nurses so that patients don't have to travel a long way to a hospital. Workers also have free health insurance with affordable medicines available to all members.

Good buy!

Divine Chocolate Ltd., the world's first Fairtrade chocolate company, was launched in 1998. The company gives the farmers from Kuapa Kokoo in Ghana (see opposite), who grow the cocoa, a 45 percent share in the company. They have a great motto: "pa pa paa," which means "the best of the best."

Customer demand is making Fairtrade chocolate more popular, and famous brands, such as Cadbury Dairy Milk bars, Green & Black's, Camino, and Theo now contain Fairtrade cocoa.

Cadbury Dairy Milk chocolate bars are sold throughout the world.

At Kavokiva, they have their own ambulance to pick up patients in their villages. This has saved many lives.

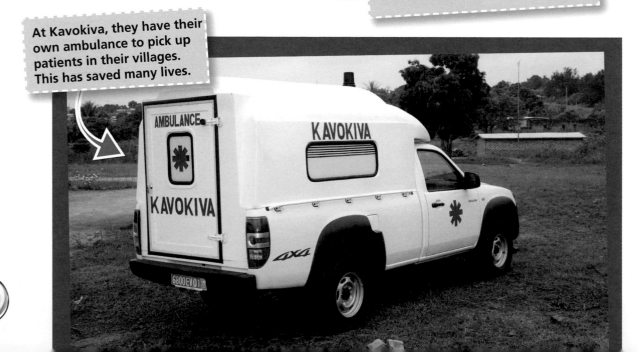

Case study: Kuapa Kokoo, Ghana

Jennifer's family belongs to the Kuapa Kokoo cooperative. Over 80,000 small-scale cocoa farmers work for this cooperative. The cocoa they sell can always be traced back to where it was grown. The cooperative knows whether the producers have been following Fairtrade practices. If the cooperative finds children working unfairly, this will be checked and stopped.

School and summer camp

Thanks to the cooperative, Jennifer can go to school in her village and attend a summer camp to learn all about fairtrade, the cocoa business, and the rights of workers. This year, she was able to try some of the chocolate made from Kuapa Kokoo cocoa beans for the very first time.

This is Jennifer at the school the Kuapa Kokoo cooperative paid for.

Bananas

The average American eats 26 pounds (12 kg) of bananas each year. Most of those are not fair trade fruit, but each year, the numbers of fairly traded bananas in store produce sections increases.

Banana plants grow on stems which are 10 to 26 feet (3 to 8 m) high. The clusters of fruit grow upside down in bunches, known as hands. Each hand contains around 10 bananas and there are 3 to 6 hands in a bunch.

Where do bananas grow?

Bananas grow in over 150 countries around the world. These countries are hot, with plenty of rainfall, because banana plants need a lot of moisture from the soil. You might have eaten bananas grown in Costa Rica, Guatemala, Colombia, Equador, the Dominican Republic, or the eastern Caribbean. Most bananas sold in grocery stores are grown on large plantations, many of them owned by large, **multinational** companies. Fair trade bananas come from small farms or cooperatives.

How do bananas grow?

Bananas grow quickly and can be **harvested** year-round. A **sucker** is planted in the ground and 8 to 12 months later, the bananas can be harvested. One slice of a **machete** chops off a heavy stem of green bananas. The bananas are washed, checked for quality, stickered, and packed into boxes.

In some plantations, workers carry whole stems of bananas on their heads or shoulders. In others, a system of pulleys saves workers' aching backs.

How do bananas get to our stores?

Green bananas have to be handled very carefully—if they bruise, they won't sell. They are transported in refrigerated ships, called reefers, and kept at a temperature of 56°F (13.3°C). It can take many days for the ship to reach the country where the bananas will be sold.

Refrigerated ships like this carry bananas and other fruit around the world. The bananas are kept cool to stop them from ripening. On arrival at their destination, the bananas are ripened in special warehouses.

Del Monte

Chemical hazard

Today, banana producers can grow two or three times as many bananas as they did in the 1960s. They do this partly with the help of **agrochemicals** that help to kill pests and diseases. But some of these chemicals are **toxic**, and can affect the health of the plantation workers. Fair trade bananas are **regulated**, to ensure the workers are not at risk from these chemicals. Because of this, Fairtrade organizations encourage **organic** farmers who use natural fertilizers.

Plastic covers

Farmers often cover their bananas with plastic bags to protect them from insects, diseases, and strong wind. In the past, the plastic was carelessly thrown away and some of the bags, which had been treated with chemicals, ended up in the rivers and polluted the water. This was bad for the environment. Now, farmers who use the FAIRTRADE Mark recycle the plastic bags because of the damage they can do to the environment.

Environment matters

In Costa Rica, pesticides from non-organic banana crops could be causing trouble. Heavy rains wash the pesticides into nearby rivers, causing pollution. As a result, local caiman populations could be under threat. A report claimed that caimans, a type of crocodile, living near non-organic banana plantations were 50 percent thinner than this healthy one.

Case study: Coobafrio co-op, Colombia, South America

In the 1990s, Albeiro Alfonso Cantillo, or Foncho, as his friends call him, got together with 19 other farmers to form a cooperative called Coobafrio. At the time, their farms were hardly bringing in enough money to feed their families. Members hoped that by selling their bananas as a group, they could ask for a better price. The cooperative proved a success, and today it has 43 farmers who employ nearly 300 workers.

The Coobafrio co-op joined Fairtrade in 2011 and now two thirds of their bananas are sold with the FAIRTRADE Mark. This means that $1 from each box is invested back into the business and the local community.

Protecting the environment

Following production methods set out by the Fairtrade organization, the co-op must make sure that local water sources are protected and waste is properly recycled. Coobafrio no longer uses chemicals on its bananas. It also provides well-paid jobs for local people, who help out with weeding.

Fairtrade has helped 82 percent of Coobafrio members to pay for school fees and uniforms for their children. Foncho thinks education is the very best way to keep his family out of poverty.

Foncho works very hard for the cooperative and for his family. He takes his daughter to university at 5:00 a.m., then returns to work on his banana farm until 6 p.m.

Reuse, recycle

Before **composting** your banana skin, use it to polish your shoes! Rub the inside of the skin all over your leather shoe, then polish it with a clean cloth. The natural oils in the banana skin help to make leather shine.

Tea

On average, people around the world drink 70,000 cups of tea every second!

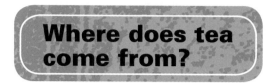

Where does tea come from?

According to legend, more than 4,800 years ago, a few tea leaves dropped into the Chinese Emperor Shennong's bowl of hot water and made the first cup of tea. Today, China is still the world's biggest producer of tea, followed closely by India, Sri Lanka, and Kenya.

How is tea produced?

The leaves of the tea shrub are handpicked by field workers throughout the year. The bags are weighed and taken to a **processing plant** nearby, where the leaves are withered, rolled, then fermented. The leaves need to be processed quickly, to make sure the quality stays high.

Workers line up to have the tea they have picked weighed. Some tea workers who are not part of a fair trade group earn less than $1 a day.

Hard workers

Most of the workers on tea plantations are children and women. They are expected to carry heavy baskets or bags on their backs, often in scorching heat. On plantations where there is no fair trade, women are usually paid less than men even though they may work longer hours. The women are often bullied and threatened by their bosses, and the children may not have access to any education.

Only the top-most leaves and shoots are picked from the tea bushes. Fair trade tea is grown without using harmful chemical fertilizers and pesticides.

Women picking tea carry heavy baskets that hold the tea leaves. They often work for hours in the hot sun.

Peanuts

Peanuts are among the world's most popular nuts. In the United States alone, around 595 million pounds (270 million kg) of peanuts are eaten each year.

Peanuts are one of the most important crops grown in the developing world.

Where do peanuts come from?

Fossils of peanut shells found in South America show that people were growing and eating peanuts more than 7,000 years ago. Explorers and traders took the peanut plant to Africa in the 1500s. By the beginning of the 1600s, peanuts were growing in China, Japan, Malaysia, and Indonesia. Although peanuts still grow in all these countries, the main producers are now China, India, and the U.S. In Africa, peanuts are known as groundnuts, because they grow underground.

How are peanuts grown and harvested?

The peanut plant grows to about 18 inches (45 cm) high. Its flowers appear above the soil, but the nuts grow under the ground. Peanuts are ready for harvesting four or five months after planting. Workers dig the plants out of the ground.

The peanuts are stripped from the plant by hand, one pod at a time.

The trouble with peanuts

Once the peanuts are gathered, they are poured into sacks, taken to be weighed, then sold to local buyers. Farmers have reported that some of these buyers use scales that are set up to cheat the farmers out of money. The local villages where farm workers live are very poor. Often there are no fresh water supplies, no hospitals or medical clinics, and no schools.

These women in India pour the peanuts into large sacks to be weighed.

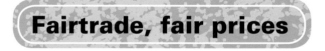

Fairtrade, fair prices

Fair trade is a way to make sure that peanut farmers get a fair price for their nuts and are not cheated when they sell them. MASFA is a Fairtrade certified association of small farmers in Malawi, Africa. By joining Fairtrade, farmers there can be confident of selling to buyers who weigh their peanuts using accurate scales. For every ton of Fairtrade peanuts sold, MASFA will receive about $93 to spend on improving the lives of their members.

Good buy! ®

FAIRTRADE

Liberation Nuts is the only farmer-owned Fairtrade company. It roasts, salts, and packages peanuts. It uses 100 percent Fairtrade ingredients whenever possible, and works closely with small-scale farmers to help them sell their nuts around the world. They work with farmers in Africa, Asia, and South America.

Case study: Mchinji, Malawi

Mary Banda and her husband owned a small peanut farm in Mchinji, Malawi. After her husband died, leaving her alone with six children, life for Mary was tough. The community in Mchinji was very poor. Mary joined MASFA and was able to get a better price for her peanuts. This has meant that Mary could send two of her children to secondary school.

Medicine and clean water

Fairtrade pays an additional sum to producers, called the Fairtrade Premium. This premium is used to fund projects that benefit the entire community, such as health care, building roads, or schools. In Mchinji, the premium is going toward building a medical shelter, improving homes, and making more **boreholes** for clean drinking water. Small changes can make a big difference to Fairtrade farmers.

Reuse, recycle

Peanut shells don't have to go to waste. They can be used to feed farm animals, or be made into cat litter.

With fair trade organizations, farmers know they will receive a fair price for their crop.

Sugar

Sugar was once called white gold, because it was a very expensive luxury. It is still one of the most valuable crops in the world.

Some fruit juices can have up to 5 teaspoons (23 g) of sugar in 1 cup (237 ml).

Sugar, sugar everywhere

Sugar is added to nearly every store-bought, ready-made food that we eat, including savory, or salty and spicy, foods. One can of soda can contain as many as 8 teaspoons (39 g) of sugar.

Where does sugar come from?

Over 176 million tons (160 million metric tons) of sugar are produced around the world every year. Sugar grows both underground as a crop called sugar beets, and above ground as a type of grass called sugar cane. The top exporters of sugar include Brazil, Thailand, France, India, Guatemala, and Mexico.

Seventy percent of sugar comes from sugar cane.

white sugar cubes

brown sugar cubes

Raw sugar crystals are brown. Sugar only turns white when it is refined.

How does sugar cane grow?

It takes about a year, a lot of sunshine, and plenty of water for sugar cane to grow well. The cane is chopped down, leaving the roots of the plant to grow again. It is then processed in a factory to extract a sugary juice. This is cleaned and thickened to make a syrup, which is then boiled to form sugar crystals. Raw sugar crystals are brown. The raw sugar is then **refined**— usually in the country where it will be sold.

Getting better

About 181 million tons (165 million metric tons) of sugar is produced each year from sugar farms in over 120 countries around the world. Many of these are small, family-run farms in very poor parts of the world. Sugar that is traded fairly means better and more stable wages for farmers. Like coffee, sugar is a fair trade staple, with fair trade organizations all over the world connecting directly from farmer to buyer. Fairly traded sugar is used in everything from sugary foods and drinks to body scrubs.

Good buy!

In 2007, Ubuntu Cola became the first organic, Fairtrade cola to be sold in the United Kingdom. As well as receiving the Fairtrade Premium, at least 15 percent of Ubuntu's profits go back to the sugar producers and their families in Malawi and Zambia to help tackle poverty.

Reuse, recycle

Sugar is one of the main ingredients in many canned drinks. Aluminum cans can be recycled again and again. It takes between six and eight weeks for the can you recycled to reappear on supermarket shelves.

In many countries, over 70 percent of all drinks cans are recycled.

Sugar—sweet rewards

Sugar is one of the most important sources of national income in Belize, accounting for almost 40 percent of exports. Farmers there have invested much of their Fairtrade Premium in improving their farming practices. By doing this, they have managed to increase their production by 30 percent.

Case study: Manduvirá, Paraguay

With the Fairtrade Premium, the Manduvirá sugar cane farmers can buy tractors and other equipment to help them plant and harvest their crop.

Working with Fairtrade has been good for the Manduvirá cooperative in Paraguay. Today, all of the co-op's sugar cane is grown organically. Farmers use warm water instead of chemicals to refine the sugar, and any organic waste is put back on the fields to help the next crop grow.

Premium benefits

At Manduvirá, half of the Fairtrade Premium is paid equally to the farmers, while the other half has been used to build a health center and provide uniforms and materials for local schools. It has also helped the community to build more homes and buy a computer and a tractor.

Honey

People have been eating honey for more than 6,000 years. Fairly traded honey is produced by small operation beekeepers, and beekeeper and honey cooperatives.

How do bees make honey?

Bees collect **nectar** from flowers and take it back to their hive, where the nectar is stored as food in the holes, or cells, of a honeycomb. In colder climates, bees seal up the cells with wax during the winter months and feed on the nectar. In warmer climates, bees produce honey year-round, but spend a lot of energy keeping their hives cool. Because most hives produce several times more honey than the bees actually need, honey can be collected for human consumption without harming the bees.

Tens of thousands of bees can live in one hive. It takes 12 bees their whole lifetime (about six weeks) to produce 1 teaspoon (5 ml) of honey.

How is honey produced?

Bees in the hive process the nectar so it turns into thick, sticky honey, which is collected and sold in stores and at markets. To collect the honey, beekeepers may use a bee smoker to puff smoke into the hive. The smoke calms the bees before the keeper opens up the hive. The beekeeper scrapes the wax from the cells of the hive, then tips out the honey. Finally, the honey is passed through a filter, and poured into jars.

Where does honey come from?

Honey is produced in many countries of the world. In the United States, people eat more honey than is produced **domestically**. So today, up to three quarters of honey eaten in the U.S. is imported from countries such as China.

Ethiopia is the largest honey producer in Africa, and Uruguay is one of South America's largest exporters, sending 9,038 tons (8,200 metric tons) of honey—worth $23.3 million—to other countries each year. Honey production provides much needed employment in rural parts of Uruguay, where many people are forced to leave home to find work in the cities.

Beekeepers wear special clothing to protect them from bee stings. The keeper puffs smoke into the hive. The smoke isn't harmful and it stops the bees from stinging.

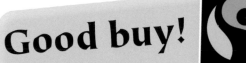

Good buy!

FAIRTRADE

Fair Trade Guatemalan HONEY from TRAIDCRAFT

In 2013, this Fairtrade raw honey was voted the best in the world for its quality at the World Beekeeping Awards. The bees that produced this jar collected their nectar from flowers that grow wild in the forest, so the honey is pesticide-free.

Case study: Cooperative Pueblo Apicola, Uruguay

In 2006, 30 small family-run beekeeping operations in Uruguay started working together as the Pueblo Apicola cooperative. In 2010, the cooperative was certified one of only 12 Fairtrade honey producers in the world. Before it existed, the beekeepers had to sell their honey to a broker who resold it for them and who paid them far less than their honey was worth.

Apicola actually means "honey producer" and the honey the cooperative produces is collected from 6,000 hives placed in 444,789 acres (180,000 hectares) of eucalyptus forest. The eucalyptus gives the honey a delicious, lemony flavor.

Loans and training

Exported honey has to meet Fairtrade standards, and the production, storage, and transportation processes are strictly monitored. However, Fairtrade has helped the farmers with loans to support their businesses, and has given special training in producing organic honey.

Buyers pay a Fairtrade Premium for Apicola's honey and the premium has been used for training workers on the cooperative. The money also pays for farmers to attend trade fairs, where they can find new markets for their produce.

Beekeepers inspect their hives regularly to make sure the bees are healthy. In summer, there can be as many as 35,000 bees in a beehive, which drops to around 5,000 in winter.

Pesticides killing bees

One third of all the food we produce relies on **pollination** by bees and other insects. One estimate claims that the work bees do each year, pollinating crops around the world, is worth $298 billion! Sadly, bees around the world are dying out. Losing bees could seriously the affect the production of 75 percent of the crops we rely on, including apples, strawberries, and tomatoes.

No one knows for certain what is causing the bees to die, but pesticides, climate change, and farming systems that produce only one crop could all be contributing to the problem.

Even wild bees can be exposed to pesticides. As natural habitats are increasingly lost, experts worry that we may start losing many of the plants that rely on bee pollination, too.

Pesticide ban

Some countries have banned pesticides that have been declared harmful to bee health. In 2013, the European Union (EU) placed a two-year ban on neonicotinoid pesticides that harm the bees' ability to navigate or fly well. Other governments are looking at pesticide bans and encouraging farming methods that are better for the environment.

Environment matters

You can help bees by planting bee-friendly flowers that are yellow, purple, blue, or white, such as daisies, cornflowers, or lavender.

Glossary

agrochemicals Chemicals used in agriculture to prevent diseases and kill insects. They can be dangerous to humans

biogas Gas fuel produced from decaying matter, such as manure or trash

borehole A hole drilled into the earth, sometimes to find safe drinking water, or to extract gas or oil

composting Letting organic waste material, such as banana skins, rot to make compost that is then used to improve the quality of the soil to help things grow better

cooperative A group of people or organizations working together and sharing any benefits or profits evenly between them

developing countries Parts of the world that are not well off, but are using their resources to build up different industries

domestically Locally, or within the same country

endangered When an animal or plant species is at serious risk of becoming extinct

estate A property where coffee, tea, rubber, or other crops are grown

Fairtrade Premium An additional sum of money paid for Fairtrade goods that is used to benefit the local community

ferment To cause a chemical change in something, such as in tea leaves as they dry

fertilizer A natural or chemical substance that is spread over soil to help plants grow

fossils The remains of animals or plants that lived on Earth millions of years ago

horticulture The growing of fruits, vegetables, or plants

harvest To gather crops at the end of the growing season

husks The dry outer covering of a seed, such as the cocoa pod

machete A knife with a long, wide, sharp blade that is used in agriculture

nectar A sweet liquid that bees collect from flowers

multinational A business or organization that operates in several different countries

organic Produced without using chemical fertilizers

pesticide A chemical used to kill insects or small animals

pollination When pollen is carried from one flower to another so seeds can be produced

processing plant A factory where food is treated to change or preserve it

refined The process that removes impurities, so the product becomes more pure, but a lot of the natural goodness is taken out of it

regulated Had rules created to control how something is done

renewable A natural resource, such as wood, that can be replaced by nature

scholarships Money awarded to students to help pay for their education

sucker A shoot growing from an existing plant

toxic Poisonous or harmful to people, wildlife, or the environment

Websites

Visit the FAIRTRADE website to find out more about Fairtrade, and the products you can buy:
www.fairtrade.net
www.fairtradeamerica.org
www.fairtrade.ca
www.fairtrade.org.uk

Read about other fair trade organizations:
wwwfairtradeusa.org
www.cftn.ca

What's so special about the Dubble chocolate bar? Find out here:
www.dubble.co.uk
Here's more about Divine chocolate:
www.divinechocolate.com

Find out about fair trade bananas here:
www.beyondthepeel.com
There's even more information about bananas here:
www.bananalink.org.uk

Discover the full story of Clipper teas here:
www.clipper-teas.com/our-story/who-we-are

Find out how Liberation Foods started, and meet some of the farmers who have benefitted from working with them:
www.chooseliberation.com

Find out about Fairtrade sugar used in Ubuntu Cola here:
www.ubuntu-trading.com/our-fairtrade-cola
In New Zealand, Karma Cola is another fair trade carbonated cola. Find out about how it started and who it's helping:
www.allgoodorganics.co.nz/karma-cola/

There's lots more about sugar here:
www.sucrose.com/lcane.html

Lots more information on Fairtrade honey here:
www.fairtrade.net/products/honey.html

Index